WHAT A WONDERFUL WORLD

Robert Thiele, George David Weiss

See trees of green, red roses too
See them bloom, for me and you
And I think to myself
What a wonderful world
See skies of blue, and clouds of white
The bright blessed day, dark sacred night
And I think to myself
What a wonderful world
The colors of the rainbow, so pretty in the sky
Are also on the faces, of people going by
See friends shaking hands, sayin', "How do you do?"
They're really sayin', "I love you."
I hear babies cryin', I watch them grow
They'll learn much more, than I'll ever know
And I think to myself
What a wonderful world
Yes, I think to myself
What a wonderful world

REFLECTION

Take a minute to remember what you were doing last Friday night when Shabbat started. Yes, this is the point where you feel the urge to go run for your phone and check your calendar, because who can remember what they were doing last Friday night? When you have it, or at least an idea, use it as a starting point to think about the past week. Think about its ups and downs and about the regular parts of this past week too. And then... Let it go. When we clear our head and heart of the hustle of the week then we can truly rest. This rest is magic because it helps us bring our best selves to the week ahead.

Where was I last Shabbat? Where was I physically and spiritually? Was I rushed, or did I savor the coming of Shabbat? What's happened in the six days past? They go so quickly that I have hardly taken notice. What kind of person was I this week? Thoughtful? Superficial? Preoccupied? Appreciative? Did I laugh? Cry? Did I tell anyone how much I love them? Did I use my week well? And what does that even mean? What lessons will I take with me into the future?

As I enter into Shabbat, I release the past week – its joys and its sorrows.
I free myself from any misgivings or guilt.
I am ready to look for new happiness and bring the best of me to new experiences during the week to come.

■ "THE RESET" AKA "SHABBAT"

According to tradition, Shabbat is not simply a good idea, but a Mitzvah. The Ten Commandments say: "Remember Shabbat, and set it apart. Six days you shall toil and do all your work, but the seventh day is the day of rest." In 11th century France, the medieval sage, Rashi, focused on a curious part of the commandment: "Six days shall you toil and do all your work. How, he asked, can you complete all your work in six days?"

Rashi understood what we still face today: That there is simply more work to get done each week than we can possibly manage. Said Rashi, "When Shabbat comes, it should seem to you as if all your work is completed, even though it isn't. You should stop thinking about work." Friday evening is designed to help us perform this magic trick, to begin to act as if our work is done.

The concept of a day of rest was also alien to many ancient people. The Greeks and Romans ridiculed this peculiar tradition, accusing ancient Jews of laziness for resting one day out of every seven. But while Shabbat is called a day of rest, it would be a mistake to think of it as a lazy day because real re is restorative. It recharges us spiritually, as well as physically. Our transition from work to rest can begin as early as Thursday, which was market day. Preparation of the Shabbat meal began, and we wished each other "Shabbat Shalom." Shabbat can free us to spend time with those we love, to savor small moments that usually pass unnoticed, freeing us to reflect on what matters most. The candles, readings, songs, and wine are all here to help set the mood, creating an atmosphere of warmth.

DAY OF REST
Sung to the tune of "Be Our Guest"
From Disney's Beauty and the Beast
Lyrics by Adam Sank

Day of rest
Day of rest
Fridays really are the best
Light the candles, say the blessings,
Let your spirit do the rest

Glass of wine,
Challah bread,
Or a dinner roll instead
We don't care if you're not Jewish
Black, white, purple, pink or bluish

Take a break
From the week
Rest your head and weary feet
'Cuz Friday nights are never second-best
Invite your friends to dine,
Serve them a lot of wine,
Day of rest, day of rest, day of rest!

Day of rest
Day of rest
Put our Shabbos to the test
Paper plates or fancy dishes
Try the tsimis – it's delicious

Tell some jokes,
Sing some songs,
On Shabbat, you can't go wrong
Spend some time at your own table
Bake a kugel if you're able

Throw your cares,
To the wind
Let tranquility begin
This weekly holiday is heaven-blessed
So come and lift your glass,
Another week has passed

Day of rest,
Day of rest,
Day of rest!

A SHABBAT REQUEST

Help us to feel peaceful this new Shabbat.
After noise, we seek quiet;
After crowds of indifferent strangers,
We seek to touch those we love
After concentration on work and responsibility,
We seek freedom to listen to our inward selves.
We open our eyes to the hidden beauties
And the infinite possibilities in the world;
We break open the gates
Of goodness and kindness
In ourselves and in others.

FRIDAY NIGHT
Sung to the tune of Billy Joel's "Piano Man"
Lyrics by Adam Sank

It's 5 o'clock on a Friday night, the work week has come to an end
As we gather together to celebrate, and spend time with our family and friends

We say, "Baruch atah Adonai" tonight, as we light the candles aflame
Things may have been kind of tough this week, but we're feeling good all the same

Oh, la la la, di da da la la, di da da da dum

Thanks for the wine, this is Friday night, thanks for the bread on Shabbat
We're together and making new memories, and our blessings, we're counting a lot!

Now Dad's favorite dish is the brisket and Mom loves the cold whitefish spread
But Aunt Marcia's become vegetarian and eats only the kugel and bread

We've invited some friends who are Protestants, and some who are Catholics, as well
Well, they're trying their best to chant Hebrew, and doing so great we could kvell

Now, the kids are giggling about something, they don't want their parents to know
And Grandma, she's snoring quite loudly after too many sips of Merlot

And the dining room sounds like a carnival as the plates and the glasses get cleared
And we smile at each other, one friend to another, and say, "Man, we are so glad we're here!"

Thanks for the wine, this is Friday night, thanks for the bread on Shabbat
We're together and making new memories, and our blessings, we're counting a lot!

TEACHING YOUR CHILDREN ABOUT GOD
Rabbi David J. Wolpe

A woman once stood before God, her heart breaking from the pain and injustice in the world. "Dear God," she cried out, "look at all the suffering, the anguish and distress in your world. Why don't you send help?"

God responded, "I did, I sent you."

LIGHTING SHABBAT CANDLES

We light two candles for the two commandments related to Shabbat – Observe and Remember. We circle our hands across the top of the candles three times, washing the light toward ourselves, and then cover our eyes as we recite the blessing. We close our eyes before the prayer, and when we open our eyes at the end of the blessing, we have entered into Shabbat.

בָּרוּךְ אַתָּה ה׳ אֱלֹהֵינוּ מֶלֶךְ הָעוֹלָם אֲשֶׁר קִדְּשָׁנוּ בְּמִצְוֹתָיו וְצִוָּנוּ לְהַדְלִיק נֵר שֶׁל שַׁבָּת. אָמֵן.

Baruch Atah Adonai, Eloheinu Melech Ha-olam, asher kid'shanu b'mitzvotav
V'tzivanu lihadlik ner, shel Shabbat. Amen.

**We praise God, Spirit of Everything, who has made us holy with your Mitzvot
and commanded us to light the Shabbat light. Amen.**

THE FINAL ANALYSIS
Kent M. Keith, adapted by Mother Teresa

- People are often unreasonable, illogical and self-centered. Forgive them anyway.
- If you are kind, people may accuse you of selfish, ulterior motives. Be kind anyway.
- If you are successful, you will win some false friends and some true enemies. Succeed anyway.
- If you are honest and frank, people may cheat you. Be honest and frank anyway.
- What you spend years building, someone could destroy overnight. Build anyway.
- If you find serenity and happiness, they may be jealous. Be happy anyway.
- The good you do today, people will often forget tomorrow. Do good anyway.
- Give the world the best you have, and it may never be enough. Give the world the best you have anyway.
- You see, in the final analysis, it was never between you and them anyway.

KIDDUSH
BLESSING OVER THE WINE

בָּרוּךְ אַתָּה ה׳ אֱלֹהֵינוּ מֶלֶךְ הָעוֹלָם בּוֹרֵא פְּרִי הַגָּפֶן.

בָּרוּךְ אַתָּה הי אֱלֹהֵינוּ מֶלֶךְ הָעוֹלָם אֲשֶׁר קִדְּשָׁנוּ בְּמִצְוֹתָיו וְרָצָה בָנוּ וְשַׁבַּת קָדְשׁוֹ בְּאַהֲבָה
וּבְרָצוֹן הִנְחִילָנוּ זִכָּרוֹן לְמַעֲשֵׂה בְרֵאשִׁית. כִּי הוּא יוֹם תְּחִלָּה לְמִקְרָאֵי קֹדֶשׁ זֵכֶר לִיצִיאַת
מִצְרָיִם. כִּי בָנוּ בָחַרְתָּ וְאוֹתָנוּ קִדַּשְׁתָּ מִכָּל הָעַמִּים וְשַׁבַּת קָדְשְׁךָ בְּאַהֲבָה וּבְרָצוֹן הִנְחַלְתָּנוּ
בָּרוּךְ אַתָּה ה׳ מְקַדֵּשׁ הַשַּׁבָּת. אָמֵן.

Baruch Atah Adonai, Eloheinu Melech Ha-olam,
Asher kid'shanu b'mitzvotav v'ratzah vanu,
V'Shabbat kodsho, b'ahavah uv'ratzon hinchilanu,
Zikaron l'ma'aseh v'reishit.
Ki hu yom t'chila, l'mikra'ei kodesh
Zecher l'tziat Mitzrayim
Ki vanu vacharta, v'otanu kidashta,
Mikol ha'Amim
V'Shabbat kodshecha
B'ahavah uv'ratzon hinchaltanu
Baruch Atah Adonai, m'kadeish HaShabbat. Amen.

And there was evening and there was morning, the sixth day.
The heavens and the earth were finished.
And on the seventh day, God ended all the work and rested.
And God blessed the seventh day.

We praise God, Spirit of Everything, creator of the fruit of the vine. Amen.

Blessed are You, who sanctifies us with commandments and has been pleased
with us. You have lovingly and willingly given us Your holy Shabbat as an
inheritance in memory of creation. The Shabbat is the first among our holy
days and remembrance of our exodus from Egypt. Indeed, You have chosen
us and willingly and lovingly given us Your holy Shabbat for an inheritance.
Blessed are You, who sanctifies the Shabbat. Amen.

BLESSINGS FOR CHILDREN

Parents and children, stand near one another. Parents put their hands on their child's head and then recite the blessing out loud.

FOR EVERY STEP ALONG THE ROAD...
ADAPTED FROM MAH TOVU'S RABBI KEN CHASEN AND RABBI YOSHI ZWEIBACK

Here with you beside me, I feel so greatly blessed.
This moment means much more than I can say.
A time to be together, a time for us to rest.
Shabbat is here.
The time has come to celebrate the day.
So I hold you close, my hands upon your head.
As I watch you growing, I smile through my tears;
Sometimes I wish you'd stay forever small.
But then I see you blossom,
And I befriend the passing years.
I love you now, I'll love you then, I love to see it all.
So I lift my voice to offer you this prayer,
for every step along the road, I will be there.

WISHES FOR MY CHILD

Our dependent and delicious newborn,
Our self-assured and adventurous youngsters,
Our rebellious yet loving teenagers...
As our children keep changing,
Growing from infancy to adulthood,
Our relationship with them keeps changing too.
But our wishes for them stay the same always.
We want them to be blessed with health and happiness;
We want them to know how much they are loved.

While in our hearts, we wish the very best
for our children every moment of every day;
We want to take this time each week to bless our children
as it encourages us to express our wishes for them out loud.
May I have the wisdom to know what blessing my child truly needs.
May my child be able to receive my blessings
and to know my love is deep and unconditional.

TRADITIONAL CHILDREN'S BLESSING

(FOR SONS) May God make you like Ephraim and Menasheh.
(FOR DAUGHTERS) May God make you like Sarah, Rebecca, Rachel and Leah.
(FOR SONS AND DAUGHTERS) May God bless you and protect you.
May God's presence shine on you and be good to you.
May God reach out to you tenderly and give you peace.

BLESSING FOR ANYONE WHO ISN'T JEWISH
('Cause we know this is a lot)
Inspired by Rabbi Janet Marder

May everyone who shares in a Jewish life feel welcome and integrated. We lovingly acknowledge the diversity of our community and are deeply grateful for the love and support you provide by opening your heart to Judaism, no matter how big or small a part it is in your day. Your presence at this Jewish experience is valued. It is not taken for granted because not everyone in this broken world will sit at a Shabbat dinner or attend a Passover Seder. We are a very small people and history has made us smaller. As we once again see a rise in hatred and hear fear in the voices of our community, we are grateful for your presence. We pray with all our hearts that all you give to the Jewish people will come back to you and fill your life with joy. Amen.

Add when reading to a family raising kids

We offer special thanks to those who are raising their sons and daughters with Jewish identity. Our children mean hope, life and future. With all our hearts, we want to thank you for your love and willingness in giving the ultimate gift to the Jewish people. Amen.

PRAYER FOR COUPLES
A JewBelong Original

There is an ancient blessing, Eishet Chayil, generally translated as A Woman of Valor that is recited in many observant Jewish homes on Shabbat. The husband recites the blessing to give honor to his wife. Sweet, right? During the blessing he compares her to rubies and compliments the cleanliness of the house, and how well she sews curtains and bakes bread. While JewBelong is all for blessing or declaring love for one another as much as possible, Eishet Chayil may not resonate the way it did back in the shtetl. JewBelong's modern version is an alternative way for all couples to show appreciation to one another. Enjoy!

(PARTNER 1)
To you, my partner, I say: "Thank you."
Thank you for being you, in all your flawed perfection
Thank you for sharing your heart and your life with me
For your laughter and your tears
Your strength and your struggles
Your certainty and your doubts
Thank you for growing with me and not away from me
For talking and for listening
For arguing and for making up
For seeing and being a light in the darkness
For all these things, I say: "Thank you."

(PARTNER 2)
To you, my partner, I ask: "Please."
Please see me as I am, in all my flawed perfection.
Please show me compassion and understanding
Through my breakdowns and breakthroughs
My triumphs and tribulations
My miracles and meltdowns
Please continue growing with me and not away from me
Seeing the goodness in my soul
The sincerity of my love
And my desire to continue building this life with you
For all these things, I ask: "Please."

(BOTH PARTNERS IN UNISON)
To you, I say: "Thank you."
To you, I ask: "Please."
To you, I pledge my love
And with God's blessing, may we enjoy the best of times together. Amen.

BLESSING TO FRIENDS AND FAMILY
Everyone around the table hold hands and read together
Adapted from Mah Tovu's Rabbi Ken Chasen and Rabbi Yoshi Zweiback

Here with you beside me, I feel so greatly blessed,
life's joys can be better when shared with friends and family.
As we sit together, feel each other's hands as a chain around the table and
enjoy the feeling of starting our Shabbat together.
As a group, let us release the past week.
Release its joys as well as its sorrows.
The last week is now part of our own personal history.
May its lessons be well-learned.
Allow us to use this Shabbat to help us rest
and prepare our mind and body for the week ahead,
and may this Shabbat be filled with joy and peace.

THE INVITATION
Oriah Mountain Dreamer

- It doesn't interest me what you do for a living.
  I want to know what you ache for and if you dare to dream of meeting your heart's longing.

- It doesn't interest me how old you are.
  I want to know if you will risk looking like a fool for love, for your dream, for the adventure of being alive.

- It doesn't interest me what planets are squaring your moon.
  I want to know if you have touched the center of your own sorrow, if you have been opened by life's
  betrayals, or have become shriveled and closed from fear of further pain.
  I want to know if you can sit with pain, mine or your own, without moving to hide it, or fade it, or fix it.

- I want to know if you can be with joy, mine or your own, if you can dance with wildness and let the
  ecstasy fill you to the tips of your fingers and toes without cautioning us to be careful, to be realistic,
  to remember the limitations of being human.

- It doesn't interest me if the story you are telling me is true.
  I want to know if you can disappoint another to be true to yourself; if you can bear the accusation of
  betrayal and not betray your own soul; if you can be faithless and therefore trustworthy.

- I want to know if you can see beauty even when it is not pretty, every day, and if you can source your
  own life from its presence

- I want to know if you can live with failure, yours and mine, and still stand at the edge of the lake and
  shout to the silver of the full moon, "Yes."

- It doesn't interest me to know where you live or how much money you have. I want to know if you
  can get up, after the night of grief and despair, weary and bruised to the bone, and do what needs to
  be done to feed the children.

- It doesn't interest me who you know or how you came to be here. I want to know if you will stand in
  the center of the fire with me and not shrink back.

- It doesn't interest me where or what or with whom you have studied. I want to know what sustains
  you, from the inside, when all else falls away.

- I want to know if you can be alone with yourself and if you truly like the company
  you keep in the empty moments.

PRAYER FOR OUR COUNTRY
Robert F. Kennedy

- Let no one be discouraged by the belief that there is nothing one person can do against the enormous array of the world's ills, misery, ignorance and violence. Few will have the greatness to bend history, but each of us can work to change a small portion of events.

- And in the total of all those acts will be written the history of a generation. It is from numberless, diverse acts of courage and belief that human history is shaped.

- Each time a person stands up for an ideal or acts to improve the lot of others or strikes out against injustice, he or she sends a tiny ripple of hope.

- Crossing each other from a million different centers of energy and daring, those ripples can build a current which can sweep down the mightiest walls of oppression and resistance.

ANOTHER PRAYER FOR OUR COUNTRY
(Because we need it)
Rabbi Ayelet Cohen

Our God and God of our ancestors, bless this country and all who dwell within it. Help us to experience the blessings of our lives and circumstances, to be vigilant, compassionate, and brave. Strengthen us when we are afraid, help us to channel our anger, so that it motivates us to action. Help us to feel our fear, so that we do not become numb. Help us to be generous with others, so that we raise each other up. Help us to be humble in our fear, knowing that as vulnerable as we feel, there are those at greater risk, and that it is our holy work to stand with them.

Help us to taste the sweetness of liberty, to not take for granted the freedoms won in generations past or in recent days, to heal and nourish our democracy, that it may be like a tree planted by the water whose roots reach down to the stream; it need not fear drought when it comes. Source of Life, guide our leaders with righteousness, strengthen their hearts, but keep them from hardening. That they may use their influence and authority to speak truth and act for justice. May all who dwell in this country share in its bounty, enjoy its freedoms, and be protected by its laws. May this nation use its power and wealth to be a voice for justice, peace, and equality for all who dwell on earth.

CHALLAH!
Sung to the tune of "Hello" By Lionel Richie
New lyrics by Adam Sank

I've been stressed out just working all week long.
And in my heart I wish to chill...
and sing some songs.
Shabbat is always waiting Friday night.
Challah! Is it you that tastes so right?

You are not like a baguette
Or a loaf of garlic bread.
God commanded us to bless you
So that no one's left unfed.
Tell me how to braid your loaves
Cuz I haven't got a clue
But let me start by saying... "Barechu."

We light the candles when the sun goes down.
And ask our friends and family members...
to gather 'round.
We bless the wine and thank God for our week.
Challah! Now it's you we're gonna eat!

Cuz you're not like sourdough.
And you're nothing like whole wheat.
You are made with eggs and sugar
As a special sabbath treat
Tell me how to braid your loaves
And I'll try it once again.
Ha-motzi lechem min ha-aretz... Amen.

HA-MOTZI

Traditionally, this blessing is made over a Challah, a traditional sweet braided bread. If you don't have a Challah, use any other bread, cracker, pizza crust, or whatever you like:

בָּרוּךְ אַתָּה ה׳ אֱלֹהֵינוּ מֶלֶךְ הָעוֹלָם הַמּוֹצִיא לֶחֶם מִן הָאָרֶץ. אָמֵן.

Baruch Atah Adonai Eloheinu Melech Ha-olam
Ha'motzi lechem min ha'aretz. Amen.

**Blessed are you, Lord our God, Spirit of the Universe
Who brings forth bread from the earth. Amen.**

DINNER DISCUSSION:

Shabbat is the perfect time to do a little soul-searching. Rather than having a dinner conversation about work, politics, or everyday things, it's a great chance to take a deeper dive and answer questions that press us to think about what's most meaningful to us. Sharing the answers out loud with friends or family can be especially transformative. Here are some questions to help you get started:

1. What makes my heart beat?
2. What project or goal, if left undone, will I most regret?
3. When do I feel that my life is most meaningful?
4. If I could change one thing about myself, what would it be?
5. What can I do to nurture close relationships in my life?
6. What is the most important decision I need to make?
7. What is something I'm proud of?
8. If I could live my life over, what would I change?
9. Are there any ideals I'd be willing to die for?
10. What do I want written on my tombstone? And how do I begin living that way now?
11. What is something you would like to share?

HOW WE REALLY GOT SHABBAT

NARRATOR (2 lines)
GOD (23 lines)
TIME TRAVELER 1 (TT1) (8 lines)
TIME TRAVELER 2 (TT2) (8 lines)
TIME TRAVELER 3 (TT3) (11 lines)
TIME TRAVELER 4 (TT4) (9 lines)
EVERYONE (2 lines)

*Casting should be done completely blind of all gender, age, and/or classic "beauty" bias, to avoid any level of prejudice.
Raw talent, on the other hand, should be considered.

NARRATOR: Welcome to Time Travel Shabbat! It's Friday night and we're on top of a mountain. Hold tight, because we are going to travel way, way, waaaay back. For the next few minutes, suspend your beliefs and disbeliefs... because we're going back to the first Shabbat ever!

EVERYONE: Whoosh!!

TT1: Hey, who are you?

GOD: Hmm. No one's ever asked me that before. Come to think of it, no one's ever asked me anything before. You can call me "God."

TT2: Well... okay, but why "God?"

GOD: "God" has a nice ring to it, don't cha think? Kind of like Cher, Madonna, Prince...

TT3 *(IN A FRANTIC VOICE):* Sure, whatever, we'll call you God, but that doesn't seem to be the most important detail at this very moment, because... **WHERE ARE WE, AND WHAT THE HECK IS GOING ON?**

GOD: You're asking me? I was just enjoying a little rest, and poof, here you are!

TT2: He's right, ya' know. We are the ones who decided to time travel.

TT3: Yeah, but I thought we'd travel to, like, George Washington cutting down the cherry tree or Woodstock – you know, something safer? But here we are standing on **THE TOP OF SOME FREEZING COLD MOUNTAIN WAY THE HECK ABOVE THE CLOUDS!**

GOD: Oh, do you like them?

TT3 (SOUNDING STRESSED): Do I like what?

GOD: These mountains. They started off as molehills... I just made 'em this week. At least I think it's a week? It's hard to keep track when you're infinite and the watch hasn't been invented yet. Anyway, everything is new.

TT4: What are you talking about?

GOD: I guess I should back up. I need a drink. Is there wine yet? I mean, I have done some **SERIOUS** renovations on this place. You should have seen it before I created the Heavens and the Earth.

TT1: So, what did you do?

GOD: Oy, where to start? Well, first there was Creation. I made everything come into being... the Heavens... the Earth... the oceans... the mountains...

TT3: Like the one we could fall from at any second? In case you haven't figured it out I'm terrified of heights.

TT4: Oh my goodness. Chill! We are not going to fall. You were saying...

GOD: Oh, yeah. So, the Heavens and the Earth part, that was Creation – before Day One.

TT1: That was before Day One?

GOD: Yup, but the thing is, I couldn't see anything. It was all darkness, and, well, this is a little embarrassing, but I'm scared of the dark. So I said, "Let there be light!" And there was light!

TT3: Great story. Now can we please get off this mountain?

TT1: Are you kidding? I want to hear more. What about Day Two?

GOD: Well, on Day Two, I made the sky.

TT2: Wait – I thought you had already made Heaven?

GOD: Yeah, but that's different from the sky. To make the sky, I had to create a barrier between the water on the ground and the moisture in the air.

TT4: This is crazy! All of it! I don't even believe in God.

GOD: I'll pretend I didn't hear that. **LIKE I ALWAYS DO.** But keep listening... you may enjoy my story.

TT4: Okay, fine keep going.

GOD: So, on Day Three I had to put everything into some kind of shape because it was a big mess. A lot like what's going on in Washington right now.

TT1: Speaking of which, how did you let that happen?

GOD: Hey, I give you the ingredients. It's up to you to cook dinner. So anyway, I got the water all together to form oceans and lakes— and then I made the water stop at the land to form continents. Oh, I almost forgot, on the Third Day I also made plants, trees and flowers. I gave every plant seeds so they could reproduce without me having to micromanage everything. This was well planned. Bumblebees pollinating peach trees doesn't just happen you know.

TT3: You're, like, smart.

TT4: Uh, ya think? He's God.

TT1: You did such a great job and then we made a huge mess.
A lot of the plants and animals have become extinct.

GOD: So I've heard ... Anyway, Day Four I made the sun, the moon and the stars.

TT2: Wait – the sun? I thought you already made light on the first day.

TT4: Stop bothering God with details.

GOD: No, it's OK. I get that question a lot. Let's just say, the whole light versus sun thing... it's beyond human understanding. Anyway, as I was saying. I made the sun. But I didn't want it to shine constantly. So that's why I made the moon.

TT1: Whoa. And then you had the earth rotate so we'd see one and then the other... that's how we get day and night, which leads us to months, years and seasons.

TT4: Show off! So... were there other creation days?

GOD: Were there other days? You're here, right? Did you ever have a tuna melt?

TT2: Of course!

GOD: Day Five! That's when I made the fish, water creatures and birds. I would have kept going, but the sun went down, so I went to sleep and the next day...

TT2: Wait, I know... us! I remember this from religious school. On Day Six you made all the animals. Then **US!** You gave humans the power to think, to reason, to speak and to run things.

TT3: The jury is still out on whether that was such a good idea.

TT1: I'll say! Do you know what's going on these days?

TT3: Shhh! God will be so disappointed!

TT4: I'm sure God knows.

GOD: Yes, I know. And yes, I am disappointed. But I gave you all the power to think for a reason.

TT4: So we could invent Flaming Hot Cheetos and YouTube?

TT3: Ugh, this is all too much for me. I'm exhausted.

GOD: Thanks for reminding me! That's the most important part!

EVERYONE: What do you mean?

GOD: After all that creation, I was **EXHAUSTED!** I really needed to rest. Hello, Canyon Ranch? But I was also happy, so I said "This is good," and I stopped working! Done! Finished! Not forever though. I called my rest, "Shabbat," which essentially means "to rest" in Hebrew.

TT3: Oh, I know about this. Resting restores us to get ready for the week ahead.

GOD: If I had family and friends, I'd hang out with them on Shabbat.

TT2: We'll be your friends. Some of us even call you "Father!"

GOD: Aww, that's nice. Thank you! Mother is fine too. I'm a feminist. Actually, I answer to anything. Except dude.

TT3: Yup, when I get off this mountain, which can't come soon enough, I will remember that Shabbat is important... and to take the time to rest and take a break from my busy life!

TT2: Absolutely. We all will. But now, we need to get back to dinner. See ya, God!

EVERYONE: Whoosh!!

NARRATOR: And so, the Time Travelers left the mountain and headed back to enjoy their dinner, which delighted Time Traveler No. 3, to say the least.

EVERYONE: Shabbat Shalom!

LASAGNA: A SHABBAT SKIT

MOM (19 lines)
DAD (6 lines)
ELLA (16 lines)
ETHAN (13 lines)
GOD (12 lines)
EVERYONE (3 lines)

> *Casting should be done completely blind of all gender, age, and/or classic "beauty" bias, to avoid any level of prejudice.*
> *Raw talent, on the other hand, should be considered.*

SETTING: Friday night at 5PM in the family's home

MOM: Oh, good, Ella, you're home!

ELLA: Ugh — today was horrible. Mr. Lippert made me read my paper in front of the entire class. And then he totally ripped it apart. He was like, "Oh, your argument is good, but you don't have enough supporting data." Whatever!

MOM: Not enough supporting data? I'm sorry, honey. I know how hard you worked on that paper.

ELLA: Ohmigod, what are you cooking? It smells awesome.

MOM: Thanks! It's a new recipe I found for vegetable lasagna!

ELLA: Well, I'll totally have a piece for breakfast tomorrow.

MOM: What do you mean? We're having it for dinner tonight.

ELLA: Oh, sorry. I'm going to a party with Nicole. She's picking me up in an hour.

MOM: No, you're not. Remember, we talked about this? It's Friday night. I'm making Shabbat dinner for the family. You can go to the party afterwards.

ELLA: Are you actually serious right now?

MOM: Yes! We just talked about this on Tuesday. We never make time to have a nice dinner together anymore and Shabbat is the perfect time to do it.

ELLA: Mom, I know you just joined Federation, but do you have to go full-on Super-Jew?

ETHAN: Who's Super-Jew? A new X-Men character?

ELLA: Yeah, Jonah Hill is playing him.
No, it's Mom. And her superpower is ruining people's Friday night plans.

ETHAN: She is good at it. Not this whole Shabbat thing again?

MOM: Yes, this whole Shabbat thing again, Ethan.

ETHAN: But Corey invited me and the guys for dinner. We're having band practice in his basement afterwards.

MOM: Isn't Corey's mom a terrible cook? Didn't she serve you that awful fish loaf last time? Anyway, it doesn't matter because you're not eating dinner at Corey's. We are having family dinner tonight and every Friday night from now on. You can do anything you want after that, but you're eating here. **Period.**

ELLA: Your band is lame, by the way.

ETHAN: You're lame!

MOM: Enough...

DAD: Hey, hey — what's all the yelling in here? Did the country guy win The Voice again?

MOM: Just your children being charming as always.
They're mad because I'm making them stay home for Shabbat dinner.

ELLA: It's not fair, Dad. I already had these plans with Nicole,
and Mom's trying to be all Golda Meir all of the sudden.

ETHAN: Golda Meir? Kate Hudson's mom?

ELLA: Um, why don't you try picking up a book once in a while?

DAD: Oh, boo hoo. You kids have it so hard — your mom's been cooking delicious food for you all afternoon, and now she's going to make you eat it. To tell you the truth, I'm envious of you guys. I wish I could stay for dinner tonight.

MOM: What? Why can't you?

DAD: Honey, you know we've been trying to finish that report all week in time for Monday's board meeting. I just came home to change, but then I'm going back to the office. We're ordering in Chinese and pulling an all-nighter.

ETHAN: So Dad gets to go have fun with his Excel spreadsheets, but we can't?

ELLA: Yeah, this is a total abuse of power. I'm meeting Nicole!

ETHAN: And I'm eating at Corey's.

MOM: NO YOU ARE NOT, AND YOU'RE NOT GOING BACK TO THE OFFICE, EITHER! YOU ARE ALL STAYING HERE AND EATING THE SHABBAT DINNER I HAVE COOKED, OR YOU WILL ALL BE WEARING VEGETABLE LASAGNA ON YOUR HEADS, SO HELP ME GOD!

EVERYONE (LOUDLY CLAPS): BOOM!

ELLA: Well, that was dramatic.

EVERYONE (CLAP AND YELL EVEN LOUDER THIS TIME): BOOM! BOOM!

GOD: Hello, oh Weinberg family!

EVERYONE: AHHHHHHHHH!!!!

MOM: Ohmigod, where is that voice coming from??

ETHAN: I think it's coming from the challah!

GOD: No, Ethan, it's not coming from the challah. And by the way, your band is kind of lame.

DAD: Listen, whoever you are... however you're doing this... just stop this right now. Leave my family alone!

GOD: I will not! For I am Adonai, King of the Universe!

ELLA: Jesus Christ!

GOD: Nope, wrong religion. Now listen, all of you: This righteous woman has prepared a vegetable lasagna for your Shabbat dinner. And even though it's incredibly dry because she left it in the oven too long...

MOM: Dammit. Not again.

GOD: ...you will sit and eat as a family and chill out!

ETHAN: Um, did God just tell us to chill out?

GOD: Yes, Ethan. I invented chilling out! Do you not remember your Bar Mitzvah? You chanted from the Book of Genesis: And on the seventh day, God finished His work, which He had made; and He rested.

ETHAN: Is that what I was chanting? I had no idea.

GOD: Oy... typical. You sounded great though. By the way, you should totally be singing lead, not Corey.

ELLA: So where does it say we have to chill out?

GOD: That's what it means to rest. Like your paper for Mr. Lippert's class, Ella. You worked all week on that. Now it's time to rest and reflect. And you, sir — if you're going to be working on a report all night, then surely it's better if you first sit down and eat with the people you love most and remind yourself what your work is for.

DAD: That's true, I guess.

GOD: Plus the Chinese place you order from is the worst.

MOM: It really is.

ETHAN: But wait, God, I thought Shabbat also meant that we're not supposed to do any work, or drive or even turn on a light switch for Friday night and all-day Saturday. So if we're going to do all that other stuff anyway, what difference does it make whether we have Shabbat dinner or not?

GOD: Because I also said, "Honor thy mother and thy father." And it is your mother's wish that you all have a special dinner together once a week. The important thing is that you do something special for Shabbat. Plus, would it kill you to spend a little quality time with your family?

ETHAN: Wow, God's kind of harsh.

ELLA: You deserve it.

MOM: Thank you, God. I really appreciate you trying to help here.

GOD: Anytime, Mom. But you really need to take that lasagna out of the oven now. It's basically shoe leather with marinara sauce at this point. I mean seriously, there's a stopwatch on your iPhone.

MOM (RUNNING TO THE OVEN): Oh, God!

GOD: Now, don't forget to chill out every Friday night. Shalom. Mic drop. I'm out.

MOM (HOLDING THE LASAGNA): Well, the lasagna is ruined. I guess you all might as well go.

DAD: No, sweetie. We're all going to stay and eat. But maybe... we'll order in Chinese.

ELLA: Let's do Empire Szechuan! They have the best cold sesame noodles. I'll just meet Nicole later.

ETHAN: I'll text Corey and tell him I'll be over in a couple hours.

MOM: This is the best Shabbat ever!

SHALOM ALEICHEM

This traditional Hebrew Psalm is often sung at the beginning of Shabbat. Loosely translated it means: Peace be unto you. May you come in peace. May you be in peace. May your departure be in peace. For He will instruct His angels on your behalf, to guard you in all your ways. The Lord will guard your going and your coming from now and for all time.

Shalom aleichem, malachei hashalom, malachei Elyon,
mimelech malchei ham'lachim, Hakadosh Baruch Hu.

Bo-achem l'shalom, malachei hashalom, malachei Elyon,
mimelech malchei ham'lachim, Hakadosh Baruch Hu.

Bar'chuni l'shalom, malachei hashalom, malachei Elyon,
mimelech malchei ham'lachim, Hakadosh Baruch Hu.

Tzeit'chem l'shalom, malachei hashalom, malachei Elyon,
mimelech malchei ham'lachim, Hakadosh Baruch Hu.

 ## GRACE AFTER THE MEAL

Baruch Atah Adonai, Eloheinu Melech ha-olam
hazan et ha'olam kulo b'tuvo b'chen b'chesed w'rachamin.
Hu noten lechem l'chol basar ki l'olam chasdo.
Uv'tuvo hagadol tamid lo chasar lanu v'al yech'sar lanu mason l'olam va'ed.
Ba'avur sh'mo hagadol ki hu zan um'farnes lakol umetiv lakol
umechin mazon l'chol b'riyotav asher bara.
Baruch Atah Adonai hazan et hakol.

**We praise God, Spirit of Everything.
You are the origin of love and compassion, the source of bread for all.
We praise God, source of food for everyone.
As it says in the Torah: When you have eaten and are satisfied,
give praise to God who has given you this good earth.
We praise God for the earth and for its sustenance.
Renew our spiritual center in our time.
May the source of peace grant peace to us,
to the Jewish people, and to the entire world.**

MORE...

THE MAYONNAISE JAR
AND TWO CUPS OF COFFEE

A professor stood before his philosophy class and had some items in front of him. When the class began, wordlessly, he picked up a very large and empty mayonnaise jar and proceeded to fill it with golf balls. He then asked the students if the jar was full. They agreed that it was.

The professor then picked up a box of pebbles and poured them into the jar. He shook the jar lightly. The pebbles rolled into the open areas between the golf balls. He then asked the students again if the jar was full. They agreed it was.

The professor next picked up a box of sand and poured it into the jar. Of course, the sand filled up everything else. He asked once more if the jar was full. The students responded with a unanimous "yes."

The professor then produced two cups of coffee from under the table and poured the entire contents into the jar, effectively filling the empty space between the sand. The students laughed.

"Now," said the professor, as the laughter subsided, "I want you to recognize that this jar represents your life. The golf balls are the important things – family, love, friends, children, health, passions... if all else was lost, your life would still be full. The pebbles are the other things that matter, like your job, house and car. The sand is everything else – the small stuff."

"If you put the sand into the jar first," he continued, "there is no room for the pebbles or the golf balls. The same goes for life. If you spend all your time and energy on the small stuff, you will never have room for the things that are important to you. So... pay attention to the things that are critical to your happiness. Play with your children, call a friend, exercise, take time to get medical checkups, take your partner out to dinner, visit someone who needs a visit. There will always be time to clean the house and fix the disposal. Take care of the golf balls first – the things that really matter. Set your priorities. The rest is just sand."

One of the students raised her hand and inquired what the coffee represented. The professor smiled. "I'm glad you asked. It just goes to show you that no matter how full your life may seem, there's always room for a couple of cups of coffee with a friend."

JOKES

KEEPING KOSHER

GOD: And remember Moses, in the laws of keeping Kosher, never cook a calf in its mother's milk. It is cruel.

MOSES: Ohhhhhh! So you are saying we should never eat milk and meat together.

GOD: No, what I'm saying is, never cook a calf in its mother's milk.

MOSES: Oh, Lord forgive my ignorance! What you are really saying is we should wait six hours after eating meat to eat milk so the two are not in our stomachs.

GOD: No, Moses, what I'm saying is, don't cook a calf in its mother's milk!!!

MOSES: Oh, Lord! Please don't strike me down for my stupidity! What you mean is we should have a separate set of dishes for milk and a separate set for meat and if we make a mistake we have to bury that dish outside...

GOD: Ah, do whatever you want....

I'M NOT GOING

One Saturday morning, a mother went in to wake her son and tell him it was time to get ready for temple, to which he replied, "I'm not going."

"Why not?" she asked.

"I'll give you two good reasons," he said. "One, they don't like me, and two, I don't like them."

His mother replied, "I'll give YOU two good reasons why you SHOULD go to temple. One, you're 54 years old, and two, you're the Rabbi."

OLD CULTURES

A Jewish man and a Chinese man were talking. The Jewish man commented upon what a wise people the Chinese are. "Yes," replied the Chinese, "Our culture is over 4,000 years old. But, you Jews are a very wise people, too." The Jewish man replied, "Yes, our culture is over 5,000 years old." The Chinese man was incredulous, "That's impossible," he replied. "Where did your people eat for a thousand years?"

FUNNY THING

The temple board president, a very pious Jew, is extremely distressed in receiving the news that his only son has converted to Christianity. He is so beside himself that he goes to talk to the Rebbe, the highest authority he knows.

He says, "Rebbe, Rebbe what have I done wrong? I brought him to Temple every day. I taught him everything that I was taught, gave him all I was given. Where, where did I go wrong?"

The Rebbe says, "Funny thing, my only son has also converted to Christianity. I, too, cannot figure out what went wrong. After all, I am the Rebbe. Surely my teachings and guidance should have been sufficient." The Rebbe continues, "There is only one thing we can do, we must speak to a higher authority still."

The Rebbe and the Board President make their way to the sanctuary and they begin to speak to G-d. They say, "Oh, Adoni, where have we gone wrong, our only sons have shunned us and converted to Christianity, what shall we do? Where did we go wrong?"

A big booming voice is heard from above to say, **"FUNNY THING!"**

Printed in the USA
CPSIA information can be obtained
at www.ICGtesting.com
LVHW071221071023
760001LV00033B/75